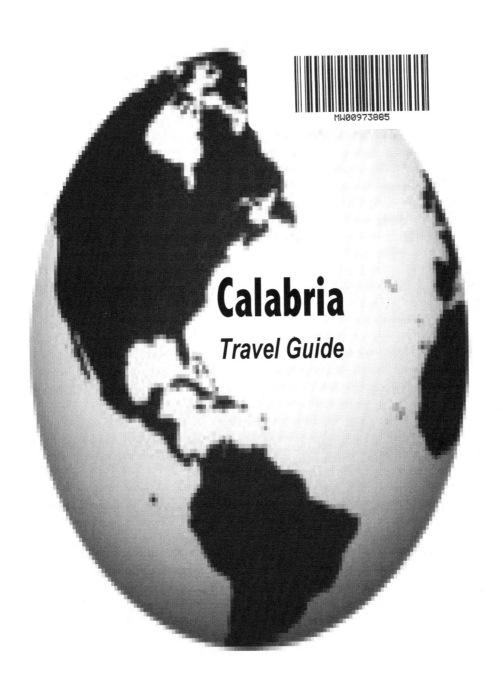

Calabria
Travel Guide

Quick Trips Series

Table of Contents

Calabria

The distinctive shape of Italy resembles a boot and Calabria is found near the toe of that boot in a sunny, tourist-friendly location.

The region's history is richly layered, with ruins and artefacts dating back as far as 600 BC. If you are interested in the ancient world, your first stop should be Reggio di Calabria, home of a fascinating pair of Greek statues known as the Bronzes of Riace.

If your historical focus is the Middle Ages, you will find a number of castles, cathedrals and other buildings to explore. Mathematicians should know that Pythagoras once resided and taught here and fans of Greek myth will want to visit the legendary haunt of the sea monster Scylla.

With a coastline of 750km, there is plenty of scope to enjoy sunbathing and watersports. Calabria offers active visitors a wide selection of activities including windsurfing, diving, swimming and canoeing to cliff jumping, rock climbing, cycling, hiking and even skiing in winter. If you wish to get close to nature, the region has no less than three national parks.

Food lovers have many reasons to visit Calabria. Rossano has one of the world's oldest liquorice factories and you can further indulge your sweet tooth with a visit to the birthplace of tartufo. Swordfish is caught and prepared all along the region's coastline. Tropea is known for a unique species of red onion and if your taste buds can appreciate fiery sensations, do not miss the annual chilli festival in Diamante or the 'nduja' sausage festival in Spilinga.

🌐 Customs & Culture

Calabria's culture is the result of a melting pot of different influences and rulers. Its earliest settlers, the Italic tribes soon formed trade alliances with visiting Greeks who built cities at Locri, Sibari, Crotone and Reggio. They were in turn supplanted by Oscan tribesmen before falling to the might of Rome. In turn, the region swayed to the influence of the Saracens, Byzantines, Lombards, Normans and Angevins.

Calabria has provided refuge to a number of ethnic minorities, who form part of the population. The most significant groups represented are Albanians, Greeks and

CALABRIA TRAVEL GUIDE

Waldensians, who originally fled religious persecution in Provence. Greek culture in particular plays a significant role. Greeks, or Grecanici have lived in Calabria for at least 2500 years and over the centuries, there has been some religious tension in response to attempts to Latinize their Greek Orthodox beliefs.

Today the majority are Byzantine Catholics, following what is also referred to as the Catholic Church of the Eastern Rite. Greek and Byzantine culture has exerted a large influence on the culture of the region. Although the dominant language spoken is standard Italian, there is a Griko version of Calabrian.

The culture and economy of Calabria has always depended heavily on the development of crafts and skills. Traditional methods of carding, spinning and weaving have survived the centuries and tapestries are made incorporating emblems and designs of Greek, Arab and Byzantine origin. The region played an important role in the silk industry and its damask work is still highly regarded.

Ceramics is another important craft practiced by the artisans of Calabria. Distinctive of the region is Seminara Ceramics, which is characterized by animalistic themes of monsters and anthromorphic animal figures, as well as masks believed to ward off the evil eye. Woodcarving, stonework and basket-making are also practiced. The small village of Bisignano produces concert grade stringed instruments.

🌏 Geography

Calabria is located in the southern part of Italy, forming the "toe" of the boot-shaped peninsula of Italy. To the north it is bounded by the region of Basilicata, with the Tyrrhenian Sea lying to the west and the Ionian Sea to the east. It is separated by the Strait of Messina from the island of Sicily. Calabria is primarily Mediterranean, but has tracts of densely forested areas and a mountainous interior.

Calabria is divided into five provinces, namely Catanzaro, Cosenza, Crotone, Vibo Valentia and Reggio Calabria. With the exception of Vibo Valentia, the other four provinces are bounded by two seas, the Ionian and the Tyrrhenian Sea. Reggio Calabria is the southern-most of these provinces. It is bounded by Vibo Valentia to the north, and by Catanzaro. The northern-most province of

CALABRIA TRAVEL GUIDE

Cosenza lies just south of Basilicata and includes the Sila Mountains, as well as Pollino National Park. Crotone lies between the Sila Mountains to the west and the Ionian Sea to the east.

The main airport of Calabria is Lamezia Terme International Airport which offers connecting flights to and from various major European cities including Brussels, Munich, Zurich, Rome, Prague, Vienna and London. There are also airports near Crotone and Reggio di Calabria. Reggio di Calabria, the largest city of the region lies at the very tip of the "toe", and is connected to Sicily via a regular ferry service. The Eurostar train service connects Reggio di Calabria to Rome, Naples and various other cities in Italy and Europe. The A3 Autostrada links Reggio di Calabria to Naples via Salerno. Calabria is well located for exploring the Aeolian Islands. The region is

prone to earthquakes.

🌍 Weather & Best Time to Visit

The coastal parts of Calabria enjoy a Mediterranean

climate, but this shifts rather quickly to a continental

climate once you reach the more mountainous parts of

the region. In the mountains, winters can get cold and

snow may occur. Rain can be expected to occur mainly

during the autumn and winter months.

July and August are the hottest months, with

temperatures on average of 31 degrees Celsius by day

and between 25 and 22 degrees Celsius by night, but the

region can experience record highs of over 40 degrees

Celsius. June typically sees day temperatures between 27

and 28 degrees Celsius and night temperatures from 17

to 22 degrees Celsius. During September and October day temperatures average around 26 and 22 degrees Celsius respectively, with Reggio di Calabria being slightly warmer.

November cools down to temperatures between 17 and 12 degrees Celsius. December, January and February are the coldest months with day temperatures between 12 and 13 degrees Celsius and night temperatures between 5 and 8 degrees Celsius. May can be pleasant with day temperatures around 23 degrees Celsius and night temperatures between 15 and 17 degrees Celsius. April is slightly cooler, with average temperatures between 19 and 13 degrees Celsius.

While the locals tend to flock to the beaches of Calabria during the height of summer, many visitors prefer to avoid the sweltering heat of the Mediterranean and book their

holidays for spring or autumn.

Sights & Activities: What to See & Do

🌍 Reggio di Calabria

Located right at the tip of the region, Reggio di Calabria is

the biggest and most populous city of the region and also

provides a convenient connecting port for tourists wishing

to visit the nearby island of Sicily, as well as the Aeolian

Islands of Lipari, Stromboli, Panarea and Vulcano (which

is famous for its therapeutic mud baths). The city's

promenade or Lungomare has been described as the most beautiful in all of Italy. It hugs the coast for 4km and is lined by palm trees and magnolias. From here, you can sometimes view the optical mirage known as the Fata Morgana. The beaches around Reggio di Calabria offer ideal conditions for kitesurfing.

Although the Romanesque features of the cathedral appear impressive, the structure was completely rebuilt after being destroyed in an earthquake in 1908. The city's main square is Piazza Italia. Music lovers may wish to visit the Museo della Strumento Musicale (http://www.mustrumu.it/), which has a collection of around 800 musical instruments from all around the world.

The number one attraction of Reggio di Calabria is the Museo Nazionale della Magna Grecia and the Bronzes of

Riace can be regarded as its main draw card. These two bronze statues are believed to portray two warriors, whom some theorize may have been Amphiaraus, a warrior poet and Tydeus, a hero and the son of the god Ares. The sculptures are muscled and lifelike and have survived virtually intact. Some of the finer details include teeth of silver, eyes crafted from ivory and glass and lips of reddish copper.

They were discovered in 1972, off the coast of Riace and and believed to have been sculpted between 460 and 430 BC. The statues serve as a reminder of the Hellenic civilization of Magna Graecia that once extended to Southern Italy. Other exhibits in the museum include a marble head of Apollo, bronze tables from the temple of Zeus at Locri Epizefiri and a collection of jewellery, bronze mirrors, coins and medals, as well as pinakes (decorative boards).

 Gerace

Gerace is located only a few kilometers from the capital Reggio Calabria, and easy to reach by train. It also lies near the resort of Locri and, according to legend, the town was originally founded by refugees from that town, after Locri was conquered by Saracens. Its beautiful panoramic views were a valuable asset to its defenders. The hill on which it lies, harbors sea fossils up to 60 million years old.

Gerace is sometimes referred to as the Florence of the South, due to a dense concentration of churches and castles within the town. The imposing Norman cathedral built of limestone is believed to be the largest in Calabria, but also of note is the Gothic style Church-convent of St

Francis of Assisi from the 13th century and a small Byzantine chapel dating back to the 10th century which was once part of the huge Norman castle. It is believed that the whole village developed around the the castle. Some of the notable mansions include Palazzo Grimaldi-Serra, Palazzo Migliaccio, Arcane Palace and Palazzo del Balzo, where you can still see the slits in the wall that were once utilized for defence.

An interesting feature of the town is the Porte del Sol or the old Sun Gate, so named because the sun's rays shine straight through the gate's arch at sunrise. Other surviving gates of old are the Porta Maggiore, Porta di Santa Lucia and Porta della Tribune. In the Borgo Maggiore quarter, you can visit the workshops of various master potters that have been carved into the mountainside. Traditional weaving and iron working are also still practiced in

Gerace. While there, sample some of the local speciality -

a cake known as 'rafioli'.

 Locri

Locri, originally Epizephyrian Locris, was an important city

of Magna Graecia and home to Zaleucus, a prominent

lawgiver of the ancient world. Dating back to around 680

BC, its most prominent ruins are the 5th century Ionic

temple of Marasa and a theatre that could seat 4500.

Locri is located in the province of Reggio di Calabria.

 Tropea

The small picturesque town of Tropea is one of Calabria

favorite tourist destinations. It lies along the Tyrrhenian

Sea, on a stretch of coastline also known as Bella Costa

(Beautiful Coast) or Costa degli Dei (the coast of the

gods). The Old Town perches on an imposing cliff top,

some 70m above the sea and, as a result, visitors can enjoy stunning views of the turquoise sea and beautiful landscape. On clear days, the volcanic island of Stromboli is visible and boat trips to the island can arranged.

Tropea's beaches offer golden sands and warm crystal clear water that is suitable for swimming. The Beach of the Rotunda can be accessed via the 'Carabinieri' staircase, a route of some 300 steps leading from Largo Gallippi, but before you hurry down, consider making use of the excellent photo opportunities offered by one of the town's six public 'balconies' or viewing points. Other beaches include Beach Island Marina, Cannon Beach and the spacious Beach of the Convent.

One of Tropea's most iconic faces is that of the Benedictine Sanctuary of Santa Maria dell'Isola, set atop a rock outcrop and surrounded by sea views. This photogenic site is a popular location for weddings, but it has carried considerable religious significance since the 4th century. The architecture is breathtaking and its facade was recently restored.

Another religious building worth visiting, is the Norman Cathedral on Via Roma. It has suffered damages from past earthquakes and is rumored to still hide unexploded bombs from World War Two, but it might be world a visit for its Gothic portals and a number of art treasures, including its icon, the Madonna of Romania. Another building of note is the Palazzo Vescovile or Bishop's Palace, which now houses Museo Diocesano, a small museum with a collection of religious art.

With its cobbled streets and palazzi dating back to the 17th and 18th century, the town's historical center is particularly well preserved. Many of its houses still feature carved granite doorways, interesting facades and exquisitely rendered frescoes. The main square is Piazza Ercole, where you will also find the town's Tourist Information Office. Soak up the peaceful atmosphere of this quaint little town with a leisurely stroll down Corso Vittorio Emanuele III, where you can stop at numerous cafes, gelaterie and restaurants. Serious foodies may want to schedule a visit for July, when the town's Red Onion festival takes place. Tropea is famous throughout Italy for its unique red onions.

 Pizzo

Although legends suggest ancient settlements by Greeks and Romans, the town Pizzo's earliest links with historical record date back the the 1300s, when it was home to a community of Basilian monks. Its cliff top location allows for spectacular panoramic views and its medieval quarter is characterized by a quaint maze of narrow streets and alleys, flanked by historical buildings. The beaches offer wide sandy bays, with plenty of umbrellas and sun loungers. The nearest beach is Pizzo Marina, which is about a five minute walk from the main piazza.

One of Pizzo's best known tourist attractions is the Piedigrotta or cave church, located about 1km outside the town. The church was carved from rock during the 17th century, probably by shipwreck survivors. During the 19th and 20th century, numerous ornamental statues were added by locals. Another landmark is Castello Murat, an old Aragonese castle dating back to 15th century. It is here that the former King of Naples, Joachim Murat was briefly imprisoned before his execution. Today, it houses the collection of the Provincial Museum Murat. Also of note is the Baroque church of St George, which dates back to 1632.

The town's culinary speciality is tartufo. This delicious dessert of ice cream enclosed in a shell of chocolate was originally invented in 1952, when the hosts of an aristocratic party at Pizzo ran out of serving cups and had to improvise. It is still popular today and can be enjoyed at various gelaterie around the beautiful central piazza. Pizzo also hosts an annual strawberry festival. The main shopping street is Via Nazionale, which is the site of a weekly street market.

 Scilla

The little town of Scilla is firmly linked to Greek mythology. It is believed to be the home of Scylla, a fearsome sea monster and spelled near disaster for Ulysses on his voyages. Today it is equally well known for a different type of marine creature - the swordfish. It has served as a base for swordfish catching excursions since historical times and traditional vessels known as "passerelle" are still used. The swordfish also provides a familiar and recurring decorative theme throughout the village.

Scilla's most prominent landmark is Castello Ruffo di Scilla. The town's strategic location right opposite the Strait of Messina has led to the presence of some fortification from as early as 500 BC but the current castle, which overlooks the beach from its hilltop location, was constructed by Calabrian dukes during the Middle Ages. It suffered some damage during the earthquake of 1783, but has been restored. From the top, you can enjoy stunning views of the Strait of Messina as well as Mount Etna in the distance. It is open to the public and admission is €1.50.

The town of Scilla is located about 22km from the largest city, Reggio di Calabria. Its beach with beautiful white sand and plenty of umbrellas is popular with tourists. The town can be divided into three distinct sections. Chianalea is the ancient fisherman's village and between its clustered houses you can still see the narrow slipways where tiny fishing boats can be drawn up. The more commercialized tourist quarter is Marina Grande, also known as Marina di Scilla. While there, be sure to pay a visit to the colorful Dali City Bar, which pays visual tribute to the Beatles. The residential neighborhood is San

Giorgio.

🌐 Amantea

The mild climate, relaxed atmosphere and beautiful

mountain and sea views of Amantea makes it a popular

base for visitors to Calabria. On clear days, the island of

Stromboli is visible. Although the waters are warm, you

should bear in mind that the sea floor descends quickly,

making it less safe for children. You may enjoy exploring

the attractive street of Corso Umberto, see the remnants

of historical buildings along Via Indipendenza or relax in

the beautiful park at Parco della Grotta.

There are several historical religious buildings of note.

The Church of San Bernardino features distinctive late

Gothic architecture and has a bell tower dating back to

1700. It is worth a visit for various art treasures including a 16th century Madonna and Child sculpture by Antonello Gagini, works depicting St Barbara and St Francis of Assisi as well as a diptych of the Annunciation by Francesco da Milano from the 1400s. The church is also the final resting place of Fra.

Antonio Scozzetta, a notable 15th century preacher. The Church of the Capuchins founded the congregation of Santa Maria di Porto Salvo in 1607 and, although its adjacent monastery was destroyed, the church has been restored. The Church of San Biagio represents Baroque architecture and includes a 19th century organ. Near Amantea, you will also find the ruins of a Byzantine fortress.

 Catanzaro

Catanzaro is known as "the city of two seas" as it is located where the eastern Ionian Sea meets the Tyrrhenian Sea in the west, offering an abundance of white beach sand. Adventurous visitors can engage in a number of water activities, such as scuba diving, wind surfing and skiing, or let the rugged domain challenge them in sports such as climbing, cycling or orienteering. Do not forget your camera, as the city and its beautiful surroundings also offers plenty of photo opportunities.

It is easy to immerse yourself in the history of the city, as a number of architectural gems remain. The Norman Cathedral dates back to the 12th century. The initial design was predominantly Gothic, but a renovation project in 1511 by Bishop Tornafranza added a Renaissance facade, which was unfortunately destroyed by an earthquake in 1638. It includes a number of beautiful art treasures such as the statue of the Madonna delle Grazie, a silver bust of San Vitaliano, the wooden statue of the Blessed Virgin of Sorrows and a 19th century painting of the Holy Family by Domenico Augimeri.

Villa Trieste, also known as Villa Margherita is the city's first public garden, located on the former grounds of the convent of Santa Chiara. It was inaugurated in 1881. Fazzari Palace in the old quarter of Giudecca was built between 1870 and 1874 by General Garibaldi and Achille Fazzari, according to the designs of Federico Andreotti.

Art lovers may want to explore a few of Catanzaro's museums. The Italian artist and poet Domenico "Mimmo" Rotella was born in the city and the Catanzaro Art Museum houses a considerable collection of his work, which creatively used décollage and was thematically associated with the Ultra-Lettrist movement. The Museo delle Carrozze Catanzaro focusses on different styles and eras of horse carriages. The Museo Provinciale exhibits notable archaeological finds, including prehistoric exhibits and ancient coins.

A beautiful and relaxing spot near Catanzaro is the Parco della Biodiversita Mediterranea, which is divided into four different zones and includes a collection of sculptures, a small carousel, a play area for children and designated fitness areas. The wildlife includes owls, hawks, peacocks, swans and turtles and there is a small train for guided tours. Admission to the park is free.

🌎 Parco Archeologico di Scolacium

Loc. Roccelletta di Borgia,

88050 Catanzaro, Italy

http://www.scolacium.it/

Parco Archeologico di Scolacium is located within the heart of an olive grove that is centuries old and a few kilometers south of Catanzaro's marina. The site can be regarded as an open-air museum and a field research center, offering the experience of archaeological exploration in progress. The ruins represent the Greek-Roman period, as well as various medieval eras, such as the times of the Normans, the Byzantines and the Angevins.

CALABRIA TRAVEL GUIDE

One significant section is the Roman amphitheater, the only facility of its kind uncovered in Calabria. Another important past structure of the complex is the Santa Maria della Roccella church, also known as the "Roccelletta", which was built during Norman rule of the region. The design of the church displayed elements of Norman Cistercian as well as Byzantine influences.

A museum displays artefacts from various periods that provide insight into the daily lives of the area's Roman and medieval residents. Some of the oldest finds date back to the 6th century BC. Exhibits include ceramics, amphorae, oil lamps, glasses, coins and other objects of stone or metal, iron tools, terracotta plates, marble statues and columns.

🌍 Vibo Valentia

Vibo Valentia offers ideal conditions for wind surfing and kite surfing, as well as underwater exploration. It is also great for cycling and the whole province attracts bird watchers and other nature lovers with its unique fauna and flora.

The city Vibo Valentia's number one attraction is the Norman-Hoehenstaufen Castle, which was built around 1000 AD with construction materials salvaged from nearby Greek temples. Although the castle was damaged in the earthquake of 1783, it has since been restored. It now houses the town museum, which exhibits various finds associated with the original Greek settlement of Hipponion.

If you are interested in historical churches, Vibo Valentia has a number of fine examples. The Church of Santa Ruba has the rather unusual feature of an oriental style cupola. The Church of Rosario features imposing Gothic architecture and impressive interior artwork. The Church of Santa Maria Maggiore e San Leoluca, a 9th century cathedral was restored with Renaissance features and has a beautiful high marble altar and a 16th century sculpture of Madonna della Neve.

Cosenza

As an important stop along the Via Polilia route, Cosenza - then known as Cosentia - flourished in Roman times and still has a few remnants of that period to show modern-day tourists. Later, it was all but destroyed in conflict between the Saracens and the Lombards and resisted Angevin rule, but also enjoyed the favor of royal patrons such as the Holy Emperor Frederick II during the 13th century and Louis III, Duke of Anjou during the 15th century. Its past has left the city with a number of historical buildings of note.

Hohenstaufen Castle was originally of Saracen construction, but has seen various additions such as an octagonal tower in the 13th century, as well as various Bourbon features and decorative emblems. Palazzo Arnone, the former court building and prison now houses the collection of the National Gallery of Cosenza. The Cathedral may date back to the 11th century, but during the 18th and 19th century it was rebuilt with prominent Baroque features and a neo-Gothic facade. Its most significant treasure is the Stauroteca, believed to contain a splinter from the Cross on which Christ was crucified. Other religious buildings include the Church of San

Domenico, Monastero delle Vergini, the church of Sant'Agostino and Giostra Vecchia.

Not all of the city's attractions are historical, though. The area from the pedestrian Corso Mazzini to Piazza Bilotti is laid out as an open-air museum and features art by Salvador Dali, Giorgio de Chirico, Mimmo Rotella, Sasha Sosno, Emilio Greco and Pietro Consagra. Adrenalin junkies may be drawn to test their mental stamina and combat skills at the War Game Arena (http://www.wargamearena.it/). You can enjoy the beautiful landscape of Calabria, while navigating your way through a tough action game scenario. If you want to enjoy a little nature without the stress, go for a hiking excursion in the pine forests around Lake Arvo or visit Silo Park or Pollina National Park.

🌐 Crotone

Myth suggests that Crotone, originally Kroton, was named after a friend and ally whom Hercules accidentally killed, but it is also associated with two other famous figures of the ancient world. Milo, the Olympian athlete was a former resident and the mathematician Pythagoras founded his school in Crotone, before he fell afoul of the city's political order. You can see plenty of physical evidence of the city's association with the Greater Greece in the Archaeological museum, which exhibits finds such as ceramics, coins, sculptures and terracotta items. Admission is €2 and the museum is closed on Mondays.

Another site connected with the ancient world is Cape Colonna, once a temple of temple of Junon or Hera Lacinia. The ruin has suffered considerable damage at the hands of pirates and also during the earthquake of 1683. Only one of its fabled 48 columns remains today.

A picturesque section of Crotone is Le Castelle, an Argonite castle ruin linked to the mainland by a narrow strip of land. There is also the 16th century castle of Charles V, which now houses the town museum and the city's cathedral, which dates back to the 9th century, but has mostly been rebuilt. Visit the Sea Environment Educational Center at the Aquarium to learn more about the region's marine life. Alternately, if you just want to cool down and relax, spend the day at the Atlantis Aqua park (http://www.atlantiskr.it/).

Nature lovers may wish to take the opportunity to explore the nearby Sila National Park. The park has one of the largest coniferous forests and offers a variety of interesting landscapes, including the Sila Grande and Sila Piccola Mountains, Lake Ariamacina and unique views of the Ionian and Tyrrhenian Seas. The nature trails offers plenty of opportunities for cycling or horse riding and a favorite activity is gather mushrooms, berries or chestnuts. Its lakes are great for fishing, canoeing or paddleboating. The wildlife population includes deer, wolves and various birds of prey.

🌍 Praia a Mare

The Sanctuary of Madonna Della Grotta (http://www.madonnadellagrotta.org/en/) consists of three caves, located about 90m above sea level and accessible via a series of steps that also allows visitors to enjoy stunning views of the Gulf of Policastrum. The arrival of its statue is shrouded in myth and the current statue is not the original one, but the spot remains a popular site of pilgrimage. It is always open to visitors.

The town of Praia a Mare developed around this place of reverence and reflection and remains peaceful, slow-paced and mostly pedestrianized. The beach offers a number of opportunities to enjoy water based activities such as white river rafting and scuba diving, as well as paragliding and cliff jumping. Dino Island, notable for its marine caves, is easily accessible from Praia a Mare. It has been declared a World Heritage Site and can be reached by paddleboat or canoe.

Another nearby attraction is the Pollino National Park. It is home to a number of rare animal and plant species and has a network of interesting caves and rock formations. The park also features a number of intriguing archaeological sites and remnants of castles, convents and other structures left behind by Albanian settlers from the 15th and 16th century.

🌀 Other Towns

Visitors are drawn to Capo Vaticano for its secluded, unspoilt beaches and coves, which offers great swimming conditions, plenty of fauna and flora and, of course, the striking granite cliffs of its cape. As the birthplace of St Francis of Paola, also known as St Francis the Fire Handler, Paola draws large numbers of religious pilgrims to its Catholic sanctuary. Stilo has a number of historic churches, as well as the Norman Castle of Roger II.

Rossano's cathedral houses a famous Greek manuscript, the Codex purpureus Rossanensis, which is believed to be over 1400 years old. It has a number of interesting religious buildings and also features one of the oldest

liquorice factories in the world. Visit its Odissea2000

Water Park (http://www.odissea2000.it/) for a day of fun and

laughter.

Budget Tips

 **Accommodation**

Grand Hotel La Tonnara

Via Tonnara, 9, 87032 Amantea, Italy

Tel: +39 0982 424590

http://www.grandhotellatonnara.it/index.php?lang=en

Although the Grand Hotel La Tonnara is located about

2km south of Amantea's center, it does offer affordable rates and a whole array of creature comforts.

Guests can enjoy the use of a swimming pool, private beach, business center with internet access, a spacious garden, restaurant, a wellness center with gym facilities, free parking and 24 hour reception. There is also a play area for children and free bicycles are available, in case you want to explore the area. All rooms are sound proofed and air-conditioned and include a plasma TV and bathroom amenities. High-speed internet is available in all areas. Accommodation begins at €39 and includes a buffet breakfast.

Hotel C'entro

Via S. Paolo 1 E, 89125 Reggio di Calabria, Italy

Tel: +39 0965 818711

http://www.hotelreggiocentro.com/english.html

Hotel C'entro is a small inn, located about 30m from the city's seaside promenade, 100m from the nearest station and 500m from the port. There is a bar/lounge and a fitness center and various water sport facilities are available. Rooms include television, a private bathroom, a safe deposit box, mini bar and hair dryer.

There is a choice of garden and sea views. Free Wi-Fi is available in all areas. Accommodation begins at €35 and includes a buffet breakfast.

Hotel Tropis

Contrada Fontana Nuova, 89861 Tropea, Italy

Located only 350m from the historical center of Tropea,

Hotel Tropis provides guests with a number of conveniences at affordable prices. While staying there, you can enjoy access to a private beach, two swimming pools, a fitness center, a spa and wellness center and 24 hour reception. There is a free shuttle service to the beach and the train station.

The hotel has wheelchair friendly facilities. Wi-Fi coverage is available in all areas free of charge. Rooms include air-conditioning and satellite TV. Accommodation begins at €45 and includes a continental buffet breakfast.

Hotel U' Bais

Via Nazionale 65, 89058 Scilla, Italy

http://www.ubais.it/en/main.html

Hotel U'Bais is about two minutes from the beach and 5

minutes from the train station in Scilla. It is furnished with

antiques, creating an atmosphere of Old World charm.

There is a restaurant and rooms include a flat screen TV,

individually controlled air-conditioning, a mini bar and free

internet access. Accommodation begins at €49.50 and

includes a buffet breakfast. Half board rates are available.

Torre Galli Resort & Restaurant

San Rocco Moccina, 1,

89862 Drapia, Italy

Tel: +39 0963 67254

http://www.torregalli.it/en/

The Calabria region also offers a number of economical

options for farm stays, if you want to enjoy the tranquillity

of rural Italy. Torre Galli is located in the Province of Vibo

Valentia and about 10 minutes drive away from Tropea.

The terrace offers sea views and there is a peaceful garden with lemon trees and plenty of flowers. There is a restaurant, a shared lounge with TV, a bar and a library.

If you wish to explore the surrounding countryside, bicycle hire can be arranged as well. All rooms include a private bathroom and free Wi-Fi coverage. Accommodation begins at €35 and includes a typical Italian breakfast, but weekly rates are available and half board and full board can be arranged.

 Places to Eat

Anema E Core Pizzo Restaurant

Prangi, Localita Marinella 75

Pizzo Calabro, 89812 Pizzo, Italy

Anema E Core offers patrons a great choice of fresh

seafood, pizza and pasta at affordable prices. A good way to start the meal is with a mixed seafood starter or an appetizer of tempura zucchini stuffed with fontina cheese and shrimp.

Some of the main courses include seafood linguine, swordfish, prawns, calamari, tagliatelle with porcini mushrooms and risotto. Portions are very generous. Service is attentive and friendly and free Wi-Fi coverage is available.

Gelateria Cesare Restaurant

Piazza Indipendenza 2, 89121

Reggio Calabria, Italy

Tel: +39 0965 181 6014

http://www.gelateriacesare.it/

There are plenty of gelaterias or ice cream parlours in the south of Italy but, for a modest green kiosk that doesn't even have any seating, Gelateria Cesare offers delicious ice cream in a startling variety of flavors. Some of the regular favorites include caramel, chocolate, hazelnut, tiramisu and fruity delights such as banana and melon. A local speciality is the bergamotta and you can also enjoy amaretto, pistachio and Greek yogurt to name a few. Instead of a cone, ask to have it served in a brioche and have it for breakfast or lunch as you stroll along the Promenade.

Civico 5 Chianalea Scilla Restaurant

Via grotte n. 5, Scilla, Italy

Swordfish is on the menu at most restaurants in Scilla, as

the region has a long history with the hunting of swordfish. At Civico 5 Chianalea Scilla Restaurant, you can enjoy beautiful sea and harbour views while eating house speciality - swordfish in a Panini - which can be prepared in the traditional way or with mint. Expect to pay around €22.00 for two portions. This small pub also offers a selection of sandwiches, wraps and cocktails.

Ristorante Pizzeria Bar Lido Calypso Restaurant

Lungomare del Convento,

89861 Tropea, Italy

Tel: 0963603322

Lido Calypso restaurant is located right on the beach and offers a selection of traditional Calabrian dishes, fresh seafood, wood-fired pizza and pasta. The service is friendly and some of the highlights include octopus salad, seafood linguine, seafood risotto and large prawns. One favorite is the nduja pizza which features a spicy pork sausage that is a regional speciality.

Il Vecchio Ulivo Restaurant

Contrada Cozzo Presta,

Cosenza, Italy

Tel: 098421494

Il Vecchio Ulivo Restaurant located on the road from Cosenza to Connici and it offers diners a rustic setting with plenty of friendly ambiance. A house speciality is 'potato' mpacchiuse, a dish native to the city of Cosenza. There are plenty of pizza choices, priced at between €3.50 and €8. Dessert options include ice cream and tiramisu.

🌐 Shopping

Fratella Marano

Via Giuseppe Garibaldi, 3,

87032 Amantea Cosenza, Italy

Tel: +39 0982 41277

http://www.fichimarano.it/

If you want to taste a selection of Calabrian figs, said to be the most delicious of all varieties, visit Fratella Marano, where you can enjoy a range of products and preserves, including figs combined with chocolate. One speciality that has stood the test of time is the "Crocette" that includes walnuts, almonds and candied orange peels. A more modern twist features figs stuffed with chilli cream or liquorice cream. The shop also stocks pralines, assorted handmade chocolates and chocolate Easter eggs.

Museum of Liquorice

Rossano

http://www.amarelli.it/

Rossano in Calabria is home to one of the oldest producers of liquorice. The Amarelli family has been making liquorice since at least 1731 and you can learn more about the family history at the Museum of Liquorice, which is housed in a 15th century stone mansion. There are documents, photographs, period clothing and everyday objects of the past, as well as a reconstruction of a 19th century shop with a range of Amarelli products displayed in the original wrapping.

The factory is next door to the museum and can be visited during the week. At the gift shop, you can stock up on edible souvenirs. Besides regular liquorice candy, some of the more innovative products include liquorice and chocolate, liquorice grappa and liqueur. You can also buy liquorice salt, liquorice sticks, powder extract, pasta, shampoo and cologne.

La Bergamotteria

69 B Torrione Street,

Reggio di Calabria

Tel: 965 20800

In ancient times, bergamot was referred to as the fruit of Aphrodite, the goddess of love. Today, it is known as green oil. The skin of the bergamot orange is used to flavor Earl Grey and Lady Grey tea and bergamot oil is used in a third of all men's fragrances and half of all women's fragrances. It was an important component of the original eau de cologne and has been used in

perfume for at least 300 years.

More than 80 percent of all bergamot is produced in

Calabria and a great place to look for all manner of

bergamot products is La Bergamotteria in Reggio di

Calabria. Some of the products in stock include a special

digestive liqueur, Liquore al Bergamotto, soap, bergamot

honey, candies and, of course, the famous Bergamot

essential oil.

Le Miniere

Via Missori 23,

89127 Reggio Calabria

Tel: +390965324305

Reggio is the birthplace of the world-renowned designer

Gianni Versace. It you are looking for fashion at bargain rate prices, try Le Miniere. You can choose from a number of well known brands such as Wrangler, Prada, Gucci, Diesel, Armani, Hugo Boss, Fendi, Lacoste, Miu Miu and, of course, Versace at up to 50 percent less than regular prices. This multi-brand warehouse type store is located conveniently near the Central Train Station.

Buying Crafts in Calabria

Making textiles and weaving are old traditional crafts in Calabria. At TessilArt, a workshop run by Mirella Leone, you can browse through a creative range of shawls (both silk and wool), carpets, embroidery, towels, table linen and napkins. TessilArt is located in Tiriolo, near the village center, in the province of Catanzaro.

CALABRIA TRAVEL GUIDE

Different towns of Calabria are known for their distinct styles of ceramics. In Gerace, for instance, you will be able to buy vases that feature hand painted scenes from Roman and Greek myth. Rossano is well known for its pitchers that are shaped to resemble fishes. Works from Squillace are known for their vivid glazing. Seminara produces apotropaic masks that are believed to ward off evil.

There is a market in Crotone on the first Sunday of every month. It takes place on the Piazza Duomo, just in front of the Basilica and there are usually around 100 stalls. Cosenza has a market on the second Sunday of the month at Largo Cimalonga. Antiques feature prominently. Soverato has a large flea market of about 50 stands on the last weekend of the month at Corso Umberto I. You will find plenty of art here.

CALABRIA TRAVEL GUIDE

Know Before You Go

 Entry Requirements

By virtue of the Schengen agreement, travellers from other countries in the European Union do not need a visa when visiting Italy. Additionally Swiss travellers are also exempt. Visitors from certain other countries such as the USA, Canada, Japan, Israel, Australia and New Zealand do not need visas if their stay in Italy does not exceed 90 days. When entering Italy you will be required to make a declaration of presence, either at the airport, or at a police station within eight days of arrival. This applies to visitors from other Schengen countries, as well as those visiting from non-Schengen countries.

Health Insurance

Citizens of other EU countries are covered for emergency health care in Italy. UK residents, as well as visitors from Switzerland are covered by the European Health Insurance Card (EHIC), which can be applied for free of charge. Visitors from non-Schengen countries will need to show proof of private health insurance that is valid for the duration of their stay in

Italy (that offers at least €37,500 coverage), as part of their visa application. No special vaccinations are required.

🌐 Travelling with Pets

Italy participates in the Pet Travel Scheme (PETS) which allows UK residents to travel with their pets without requiring quarantine upon re-entry. Certain conditions will need to be met. The animal will have to be microchipped and up to date on rabies vaccinations. In the case of dogs, a vaccination against canine distemper is also required by the Italian authorities. When travelling from the USA, your pet will need to be micro-chipped or marked with an identifying tattoo and up to date on rabies vaccinations. An EU Annex IV Veterinary Certificate for Italy will need to be issued by an accredited veterinarian. On arrival in Italy, you can apply for an EU pet passport to ease your travel in other EU countries.

🌐 Airports

Fiumicino – Leonardo da Vinci International Airport (FCO) is one of the busiest airports in Europe and the main international airport of Italy. It is located about 35km southwest of the historical quarter of Rome. Terminal 5 is used for trans-Atlantic and international flights, while Terminals 1, 2 and 3 serve mainly for domestic flights and medium haul flights to other European destinations. Before Leonardo da Vinci replaced it, the **Ciampino–G. B. Pastine International Airport** (CIA) was the main international airport servicing Rome and Italy. It is one of the oldest airports in the country still in use. Although it declined in importance, budget airlines such as Ryanair boosted its air traffic in recent years. The airport is used by Wizz Air, V Bird, Helvetic, Transavia Airlines, Sterling, Ryanair, Thomsonfly, EasyJet, Air Berlin, Hapag-Lloyd Express and Carpatair.

Milan Malpensa Airport (MXP) is the largest of the three airports serving the city of Milan. Located about 40km northwest of Milan's city center, it connects travellers to the regions of Lombardy, Piedmont and Liguria. **Milan Linate Airport** (LIN) is Milan's second international airport. **Venice Marco Polo Airport** (VCE) provides access to the charms of Venice. **Olbia Costa Smeralda Airport** (OLB) is located near Olbia, Sardinia. Main regional airports are **Guglielmo Marconi Airport** (BLQ), an international airport servicing the region of Bologna, **Capodichino Airport** at Naples (NAP), **Pisa International Airport** (PSA), formerly Galileo Galilei Airport, the main airport serving Tuscany, **Sandro Pertini Airport** near Turin (TRN), **Cristoforo Colombo** in Genoa (GOA), **Punta Raisi Airport** in Palermo (PMO), **Vincenzo Bellini Airport** in Catania (CTA) and **Palese Airport** in Bari (BRI).

🌍 Airlines

Alitalia is the flag carrier and national airline of Italy. It has a subsidiary, Alitalia CityLiner, which operates short-haul regional flights. Air Dolomiti is a regional Italian based subsidiary of of the Lufthansa Group. Meridiana is a privately owned airline based at Olbia in Sardinia.

Fiumicino - Leonardo da Vinci International Airport serves as the main hub for Alitalia, which has secondary hubs at Milan Linate and Milan Malpensa Airport. Alitalia CityLiner uses Fiumicino – Leonardo da Vinci International Airport as main hub and has secondary hubs at Milan-Linate, Naples and Trieste. Fiumicino – Leonardo da Vinci International Airport is also one of two primary hubs used by the budget Spanish airline Vueling. Milan Malpensa Airport is one of the largest bases for the British budget airline EasyJet. Venice Airport serves as an Italian base for the Spanish budget airline, Volotea, which provides connections mainly to other destinations in Europe. Olbia Costa Smeralda Airport (OLB), located near Olbia, Sardinia is the primary base of Meridiana, a private Italian Airline in partnership with Air Italia and Fly Egypt.

🌍 Currency

Italy's currency is the Euro. It is issued in notes in denominations of €500, €200, €100, €50, €20, €10 and €5.

Coins are issued in denominations of €2, €1, 50c, 20c, 10c, 5c, 2c and 1c.

🌐 Banking & ATMs

Using ATMs or Bancomats, as they are known in Italy, to withdraw money is simple if your ATM card is compatible with the MasterCard/Cirrus or Visa/Plus networks. There is a €250 limit on daily withdrawals. Italian machines are configured for 4-digit PIN numbers, although some machines will be able to handle longer PIN numbers. Bear in mind some Bancomats can run out of cash over weekends and that the more remote villages may not have adequate banking facilities so plan ahead.

🌐 Credit Cards

Credit cards are valid tender in most Italian businesses. While Visa and MasterCard are accepted universally, most tourist oriented businesses also accept American Express and Diners Club. Credit cards issued in Europe are smart cards that that are fitted with a microchip and require a PIN for each transaction. This means that a few ticket machines, self-service vendors and other businesses may not be configured to accept the older magnetic strip credit cards. Do remember to advise your bank or credit card company of your travel plans before leaving.

🌍 Tourist Taxes

Tourist tax varies from city to city, as each municipality sets its own rate. The money is collected by your accommodation and depends on the standard of accommodation. A five star establishment will levy a higher amount than a four star or three star establishment. You can expect to pay somewhere between €1 and €7 per night, with popular destinations like Rome, Venice, Milan and Florence charging a higher overall rate. In some regions, the rate is also adjusted seasonally. Children are usually exempt until at least the age of 10 and sometimes up to the age of 18. In certain areas, disabled persons and their companions also qualify for discounted rates. Tourist tax is payable directly to the hotel or guesthouse before the end of your stay.

🌍 Reclaiming VAT

If you are not from the European Union, you can claim back VAT (Value Added Tax) paid on your purchases in Italy. The VAT rate in Italy is 21 percent and this can be claimed back on your purchases if certain conditions are met. The merchant needs to be partnered with a VAT refund program. This will be indicated if the shop displays a "Tax Free" sign. The shop assistant will fill out a form for reclaiming VAT. When you submit this at the airport, you will receive your refund.

🌐 Tipping Policy

If your bill includes the phrase "coperto e servizio", that means that a service charge or tip is already included. Most waiting staff in Italy are salaried workers, but if the service is excellent, a few euros extra would be appreciated.

🌐 Mobile Phones

Most EU countries, including Italy use the GSM mobile service. This means that most UK phones and some US and Canadian phones and mobile devices will work in Italy. While you could check with your service provider about coverage before you leave, using your own service in roaming mode will involve additional costs. The alternative is to purchase an Italian SIM card to use during your stay in Italy.

Italy has four mobile networks. They are TIM, Wind, Vodafone and Tre (3) and they all provide pre-paid services. TIM offers two tourist options, both priced at €20 (+ €10 for the SIM card) with a choice of two packages - 2Gb data, plus 200 minutes call time or internet access only with a data allowance of 5Gb. Vodafone, Italy's second largest network offers a Vodafone Holiday package including SIM card for €30. They also offer the cheapest roaming rates. Wind offers an Italian Tourist pass for €20 which includes 100 minutes call time and 2Gb data and can be extended with a restart option for an extra €10.

To purchase a local SIM card, you will need to show your passport or some other form of identification and provide your residential details in Italy. By law, SIM registration is required prior to activation. Most Italian SIM cards expire after a 90 day period of inactivity. When dialling internationally, remember to use the (+) sign and the code of the country you are connecting to.

 Dialling Code

The international dialling code for Italy is +39.

Emergency Numbers

Police: 113

Fire: 115

Ambulance: 118

MasterCard: 800 789 525

Visa: 800 819 014

Public Holidays

1 January: New Year's Day (Capodanno)

6 January: Day of the Epiphany (Epifania)

March-April: Easter Monday (Lunedì dell'Angelo or Pasquetta)

25 April: Liberation Day (Festa della Liberazione)

1 May: International Worker's Day (Festa del Lavoro / Festa dei Lavoratori)

2 June: Republic Day (Festa della Repubblica)

15 August: Assumption Day (Ferragosto / Assunta)

1 November: All Saints Day (Tutti i santi / Ognissanti)

8 December: Immaculate Conception (Immacolata Concezione / Immacolata)

25 December: Christmas Day (Natale)

26 December: St Stephen's Day (Santo Stefano)

A number of Saints days are observed regionally throughout the year.

🌏 Time Zone

Italy falls in the Central European Time Zone. This can be calculated as Greenwich Mean Time/Coordinated Universal Time (GMT/UTC) +2; Eastern Standard Time (North America) -6; Pacific Standard Time (North America) -9.

🌏 Daylight Savings Time

Clocks are set forward one hour on 29 March and set back one hour on 25 October for Daylight Savings Time.

🌐 School Holidays

The academic year begins in mid September and ends in mid June. The summer holiday is from mid June to mid September, although the exact times may vary according to region. There are short breaks around Christmas and New Year and also during Easter. Some regions such as Venice and Trentino have an additional break during February for the carnival season.

🌐 Trading Hours

Trading hours for the majority of shops are from 9am to 12.30pm and then again from 3.30pm to 7.30pm, although in some areas, the second shift may be from 4pm to 8pm instead. The period between 1pm and 4pm is known in Italy as the *riposo*. Large department shops and malls tend to be open from 9am to 9pm, from Monday to Saturday. Post offices are open from 8.30am to 1.30pm from Monday to Saturday. Most shops and many restaurants are closed on Sundays. Banking hours are from 8.30am to 1.30pm and then again from 3pm to 4pm, Monday to Friday. Most restaurants are open from noon till 2.30pm and then again from 7pm till 11pm or midnight, depending on the establishment. Nightclubs open around 10pm, but only liven up after midnight. Closing times vary, but will generally be between 2am and 4am. Museum hours vary, although major sights tend to be open continuously and often up to 7.30pm. Many museums are closed on Mondays.

🌍 Driving Laws

The Italians drive on the right hand side of the road. A driver's licence from any of the European Union member countries is valid in Italy. Visitors from non-EU countries will require an International Driving Permit that must remain current throughout the duration of their stay in Italy.

The speed limit on Italy's autostrade is 130km per hour and 110km per hour on main extra-urban roads, but this is reduced by 20km to 110km and 90km respectively in rainy weather. On secondary extra-urban roads, the speed limit is 90km per hour; on urban highways, it is 70km per hour and on urban roads, the speed limit is 50km per hour. You are not allowed to drive in the ZTL or Limited Traffic Zone (or *zona traffico limitato* in Italian) unless you have a special permit.

Visitors to Italy are allowed to drive their own non-Italian vehicles in the country for a period of up to six months. After this, they will be required to obtain Italian registration with Italian licence plates. Italy has very strict laws against driving under the influence of alcohol. The blood alcohol limit is 0.05 and drivers caught above the limit face penalties such as fines of up to €6000, confiscation of their vehicles, suspension of their licenses and imprisonment of up to 6 months. Breathalyzer tests are routine at accident scenes.

🌐 Drinking Laws

The legal drinking age in Italy is 16. While drinking in public spaces is allowed, public drunkenness is not tolerated. Alcohol is sold in bars, wine shops, liquor stores and grocery shops.

🌐 Smoking Laws

In 2005, Italy implemented a policy banning smoking from public places such as bars, restaurants, nightclubs and working places, limiting it to specially designated smoking rooms. Further legislation banning smoking from parks, beaches and stadiums is being explored.

🌐 Electricity

Electricity: 220 volts

Frequency: 50 Hz

Italian electricity sockets are compatible with the Type L plugs, a plug that features three round pins or prongs, arranged in a straight line. An alternate is the two-pronged Type C Euro adaptor. If travelling from the USA, you will need a power converter or transformer to convert the voltage from 220 to 110, to avoid damage to your appliances. The latest models of many laptops, camcorders, mobile phones and digital cameras are dual-voltage with a built in converter.

🌐 Tourist Information (TI)

There are tourist information (TI) desks at each of the terminals of the Leonardo da Vinci International Airport, as well as interactive Information kiosks with the latest touch-screen technology. In Rome, the tourist office can be found at 5 Via Parigi, near the Termini Station and it is identified as APT, which stands for Azienda provinciale del Turismo. Free maps and brochures of current events are available from tourist kiosks.

Several of the more tourist-oriented regions of Italy offer tourist cards that include admission to most of the city's attractions. While these cards are not free, some offer great value for money. A variety of tourism apps are also available online.

🌐 Food & Drink

Pasta is a central element of many typically Italian dishes, but there are regional varieties and different types of pasta are matched to different sauces. Well known pasta dishes such as lasagne and bolognaise originated in Bologna. Stuffed pasta is popular in the northern part of Italy, while the abundance of seafood and olives influences southern Italian cuisine. As far as pizza goes, the Italians differentiate between the thicker Neapolitan pizza and the thin crust Roman pizza, as well as white pizza, also known as focaccia and tomato based pizza. Other standards include minestrone soup, risotto, polenta and a variety of cheeses, hams, sausages and salamis. If you are on a budget, consider snacking on stuzzichini with a few drinks during happy hour which is often between 7 and 9pm. The fare can include salami, cheeses, cured meat, mini pizzas, bread, vegetables, pastries or pate. In Italy, Parmesan refers only to cheese originating from the area surrounding Parma. Favorites desserts include tiramisu or Italian gelato.

Italians enjoy relaxing to aperitifs before they settle down to a meal and their favorites are Campari, Aperol or Negroni, the famous Italian cocktail. Wine is enjoyed with dinner. Italy is particularly famous for its red wines. The best known wine regions are Piedmont, which produces robust and dry reds, Tuscany and Alto Adige, where Alpine soil adds a distinctive acidity. After the meal, they settle down to a glass of limoncello, the country's most popular liqueur, or grappa, which is distilled from grape seeds and stems, as digestive. Other options in this class include a nut liqueur, nocino, strawberry based Fragolino Veneto or herbal digestives like gineprino, laurino or mirto. Italians are also fond of coffee. Espresso is drunk through throughout the day, but cappuccino is considered a morning drink. The most popular beers in Italy are Peroni and Moretti.

 Websites

http://vistoperitalia.esteri.it/home/en

This is the website of the Consulate General of Italy. Here you can look up whether you will need a visa and also process your application online.

http://www.italia.it/en/home.html

The official website of Italian tourism

http://www.italia.it/en/useful-info/mobile-apps.html

Select the region of your choice to download a useful mobile app to your phone.

http://www.italylogue.com/tourism

http://italiantourism.com/index.html

http://www.reidsitaly.com/

http://wikitravel.org/en/Italy

https://www.summerinitaly.com/

http://www.accessibleitalianholiday.com/

Planning Italian vacations around the needs of disabled tourists.

Made in the USA
Middletown, DE
23 May 2017